Schaum Making Music Method

Primer Level

By John W. Schaum
Revised and Edited by Wesley Schaum

FOREWORD

This book is designed for beginning piano students age 7 and up. It uses the well-proven middle-C approach. This edition is a **new beginning**. Based on the pedagogical concepts of John W. Schaum, it has major changes in presentation sequence and format – incorporating evaluations by several independent teachers with dozens of years of teaching experience.

Special care is devoted to the important lessons during the first month of study. Clear explanations and illustrations of musical fundamentals provide ease of use for the teacher. The text is **carefully worded** so it can be readily understood by young students. **Self help** is encouraged by the inclusion of a *Reference Page* and a *Music Dictionary* with unique definitions of very basic terms, cross referenced with pages in the book.

Note reading proficiency is promoted by an emphasis on **training the eyes** to recognize various melodic intervals, up and down. The student is introduced to rudimentary **form and analysis** by learning to identify and recognize various melodic patterns and rhythmic patterns, indicated by a slur.

The Schaum *Making Music Method* consists of **six books**, from Primer Level through Level 5.

NOTE TO PARENTS

The first several months of lessons establish important habits for a student. Even if you know little about music, you can be a big help. Helping to **establish the habit of daily practice** can be of immense value. The best plan is to set a regular time for practice each day (except weekends and holidays). If practice is missed on a weekday, it could be made up during the weekend. Just five to ten minutes per practice session is sufficient at first.

Practice is an **opportunity for "quality time"** with your child, even if it is simply sitting nearby and listening attentively. Try to structure household events to avoid interruptions and distractions during practice. You could assist with reading the explanations and directions in this book when needed. The teacher may suggest other ways in which you can help.

Schaum Publications, Inc.

EXCLUSIVELY DISTRIBUTED BY

HAL•LEONARD®
CORPORATION
7777 W. BLUEMOUND RD. P.O. BOX 13819 MILWAUKEE, WI 53213

CONTENTS

NOTE TO TEACHERS

Important **musical fundamentals** are found on pages 3 through 15. It is recommended that these pages be presented several at a time during the first few weeks of lessons. The materials on these pages are intended to help you to teach with greater ease and efficiency. Explanations are kept short and use language that is easy for the student to understand. Parents should be encouraged to review these pages with their child at home.

Many pages include **workbook assignments** to reinforce the concepts presented. It is not necessary for the student to complete the written work during lesson time. Instead, be sure that the directions are understood and let the written part be done as homework.

Music Notation Games, on page 49, may be started with the first piece of music on page 16.

Duet accompaniments are included starting on page 16. This is done to help students gain a feeling for a steady beat. Valuable ear training is acquired from the ensemble experience of playing with another person.

Simple **dynamic markings** are introduced early to get students to listen carefully as they play and to train their sense of touch.

Finger numbers are used sparingly to avoid reading numbers instead of notes.

Hand and Seating Postions

Hand Position

1. *Fingers should be curved* so that the *tip* of each finger, just behind the fingernail, touches the piano key (except the thumb). Grasping a tennis ball will give a feeling of the correct finger curve.

2. Fingertips should be kept close to the keys when playing. Long fingernails make this difficult.

Wrists, Arms and Elbows

1. The back of the hand should be almost flat (horizontal).

2. The wrist should have very little up-and-down movement when playing.

3. There should be only small movements of the forearm and elbow.

Posture and Seating Position

1. Sit *at the middle* of the keyboard. (The piano factory name is in the middle.)

2. Sit up *comfortably straight*, so that shoulders are not hunched forward.

3. Ideally, the *bench or chair height* should enable the underside of the fore-arms to be nearly level with the keyboard. A seat cushion could be added, if needed.

4. It is better *not to sit too close* to the key-board. The seated position should allow space for hands and arms to move freely.

SUGGESTED CURRICULUM

Teacher's Note: This method book is intended to be part of a lesson plan that also includes *music theory*, *technic* and *repertoire* development. The following are among many books available for the primer level:

Schaum THEORY WORKBOOK, Primer Level (catalog #02-80)
Schaum FINGERPOWER®, Primer Level (catalog #04-20)
Schaum GOLD STAR FAVORITES, Primer Level (catalog #03-60)

For complete descriptions and contents of these books see our web site: **www.schaumpiano.net**

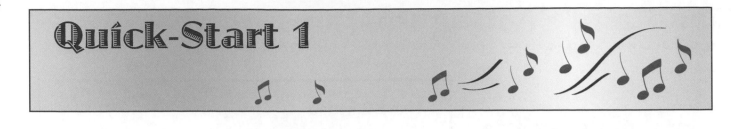

Quick-Start 1

Before starting to play, you need to know a few things about the piano keyboard and how music is written. Your teacher will help you with these Quick Start pages.

Groups of Black Keys

The piano keyboard has groups of 2 black keys and 3 black keys which alternate.
The black keys help you to find the letter names of the white keys.

*DIRECTIONS: Write the number 2 or 3 in the box above each black key group in the diagram below. The two numbers printed in the boxes are a sample.

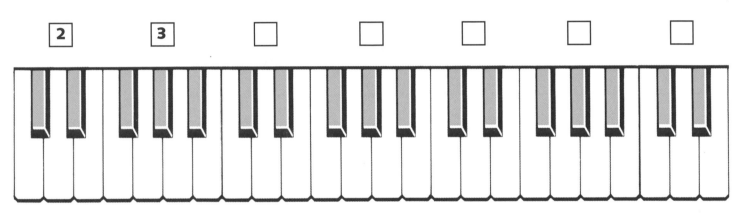

Musical Alphabet

In music, only the letters A through G are used. This is called the ***musical alphabet***.
These seven letters – A-B-C-D-E-F-G – are repeated over and over on the white keys of the piano, as shown on the keyboard below.

*DIRECTIONS: Write letters for the remaining white keys on the diagram below. Notice how the same letters match up with each black key group.

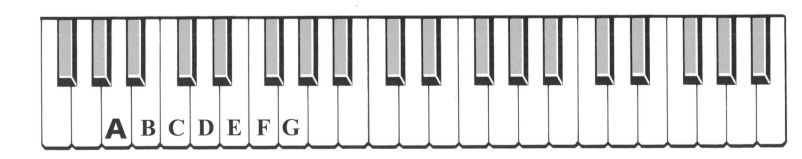

*Teacher's Note: The concepts on this page and on pages 5-6-7 may be explained at the first lesson.
The written work may be started at the lesson and finished as homework.

Quick-Start 2

White Key Names in 2-Black Key Groups

See how the letter D is found *in the middle of the 2 black keys*.
When you can find D, you will be able to easily find C and E on the keyboard.

DIRECTIONS: On the keyboard below, write the letter D in each group of 2 black keys. Then write the letters C and E on the white keys next to each D. Letters printed on the keyboard are samples.

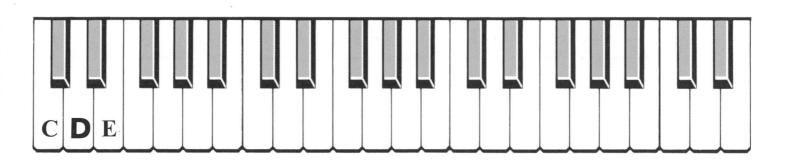

White Key Names in 3-Black Key Groups

Notice where the letter A is found in a group of 3 black keys.
When you can find A, you can also find the letters F, G and B on the keyboard.

DIRECTIONS: On the keyboard below, write the letter A in each group of 3 black keys. Then write the letters F, G and B on the white keys next to each A. Letters printed on the keyboard are samples.

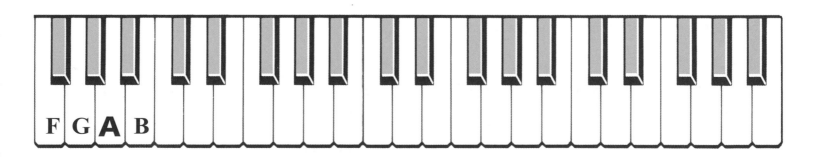

Teacher's Note: Schaum's *Theory Workbook, Primer Level* (catalog #02-80) provides additional written work that coordinates with this book to reinforce the learning elements. It may be started at the first lesson.

Quick-Start 3

Up and Down at the Keyboard

The sounds on a piano become *higher* as you move to the *right* on the keyboard.
    Going UP on the keyboard means moving to the RIGHT.

The sounds on a piano become *lower* as you move to the *left* on the keyboard.
    Going DOWN on the keyboard means moving to the LEFT.

DIRECTIONS:

1. Play all of the A's on the keyboard, going UP. Start at the *left end* of the keyboard.
Look for groups of *3 black keys* to help locate the A's.
Listen carefully as you play. Notice that the sounds get *higher* as you go to the right.

2. Play all of the D's on the keyboard, going DOWN. Start at the *right end* of the keyboard.
Look for groups of *2 black keys*. Notice that the sounds get *lower* as you go to the left.

3. For extra practice, play all of the A's going DOWN. Then play all of the D's going UP.

Musical Alphabet Forward and Backward

When going UP on the keyboard, the musical alphabet moves *forward*.
When going DOWN, the musical alphabet moves *backward*.

DIRECTIONS: Write the word UP or DOWN in the box next to each arrow below. Then write the letters of the musical alphabet, starting with the printed letter, in the direction shown by the arrow. The first keyboard is printed as a sample.

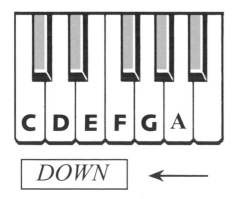

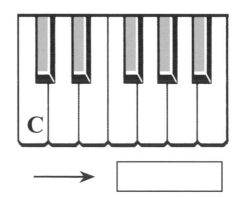

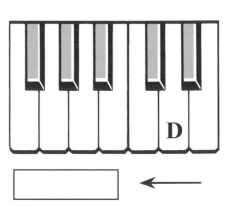

Finger Numbers

The fingers of each hand are numbered as shown below. Notice that in BOTH hands:

The *thumb* is number **1**.
The *middle* finger is number **3**.
The *smallest* finger is number **5**.

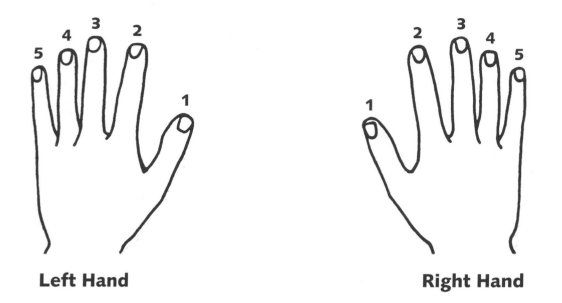

Left Hand   **Right Hand**

Fingering is important when playing the piano.
Correct fingering makes it easier to play and makes the music move smoothly.

DIRECTIONS: Write the word "right" or "left" on the line under each hand shown below.
Then write the correct finger number in the box above each finger.

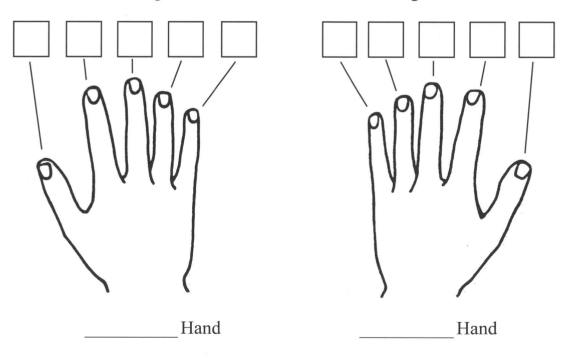

_____ Hand   _____ Hand

Teacher's Note: It would be beneficial to have the student find and play different letters on the keyboard with various fingers. For example, the student could play all of the A's using the 2nd finger of the right hand. Next, all the A's could be played with the 3rd finger of the left hand. Then the D's could be played with different fingers of each hand, etc. This shows the student that *any finger* may be used to play *any note*.

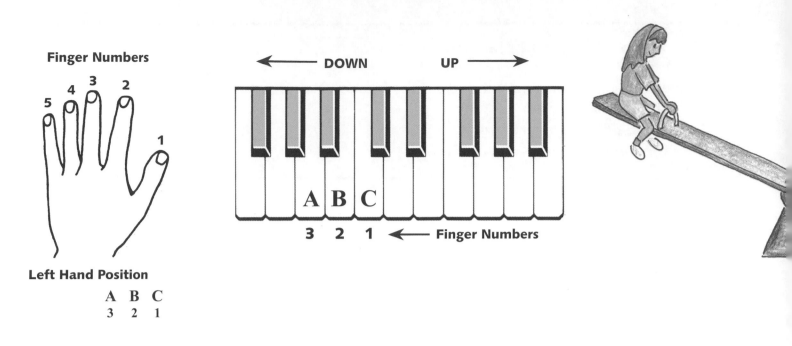

Finger Numbers

Left Hand Position

A B C
3 2 1

Left Hand Goes Up

*DIRECTIONS: Place left hand fingers on the keyboard using the position shown in the diagram above. Say the letter names out loud as you play the line below. Say the word "rest" for each dash (–). Try playing this melody starting on three different A's on the keyboard.

| A   A   A   – | B   B   B   – | C   C   C   – |

Musical alphabet goes *forward* as you go UP on the keyboard.

Left Hand Goes Down

DIRECTIONS: Place left hand fingers on the keyboard using the position shown in the diagram above. Say the letter names out loud as you play the line below. Say the word "rest" for each dash (–). Try playing this melody starting on three different C's on the keyboard.

| C   C   C   – | B   B   B   – | A   A   A   – |

Musical alphabet goes *backward* as you go DOWN on the keyboard.

Left Hand Up and Down

DIRECTIONS: Say the letter names out loud as you play. Say the word "rest" for each dash (–). Try playing this melody starting on three different A's on the keyboard.

| A   A   B   B | C   C   C   – | C   C   B   B | A   A   A   – |

Alphabet goes *forward* as you go UP.   Alphabet goes *backward* as you go DOWN.

*Teacher's Note: The left hand is presented first to start with the letters A-B-C, the first three letters in the musical alphabet. Vertical lines correspond to measure bar lines in 4/4 time. The dash is equivalent to a quarter rest. (*Do NOT explain* bar lines, measures and rests here. These will be presented later in the book.) Demonstrate a steady beat by clapping the rhythm. Have the student clap with you to gain a feeling for a steady beat.

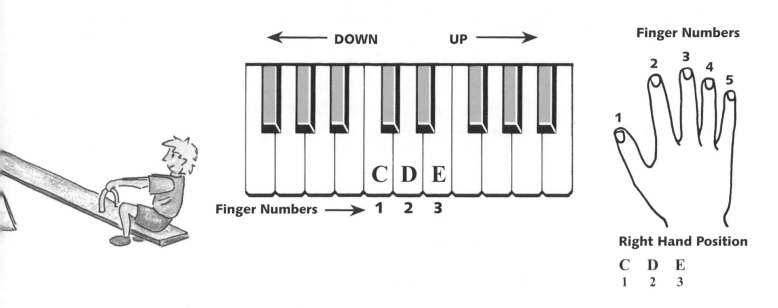

Right Hand Goes Up

DIRECTIONS: Place right hand fingers on the keyboard using the position shown in the diagram above. Say the letter names out loud as you play the line below. Say the word "rest" for each dash (–). Try playing this melody starting on three different C's on the keyboard.

| C   C   C   – | D   D   D – | E   E   E   – |

Musical alphabet goes *forward* as you go UP on the keyboard.

Right Hand Goes Down

DIRECTIONS: Place right hand fingers on the keyboard using the position shown in the diagram above. Say the letter names out loud as you play the line below. Say the word "rest" for each dash (–). Try playing this melody starting on three different E's on the keyboard.

| E   E   E   – | D   D   D – | C   C   C   – |

Musical alphabet goes *backward* as you go DOWN on the keyboard.

Right Hand Up and Down

DIRECTIONS: Say the letter names out loud as you play. Say the word "rest" for each dash (–). Try playing this melody starting on three different C's on the keyboard.

| C   C   D   D | E   E   E   – | E   E   D   D | C   C   C   – |

Alphabet goes *forward* as you go UP.   Alphabet goes *backward* as you go DOWN.

Words Used in Music

Your teacher will explain these words with the first pieces you will be playing.
You may also look at the Reference Page on the front inside cover.

Staff – Group of five equally spaced horizontal lines.
Music notes are placed on or near the staff.

Bar Line – Vertical line placed in the staff.

Measure – Part of the staff between two bar lines.

Staff

Bar Line

Measure

Clef – Sign placed at the left end of a staff.

Treble Clef – The *upper* part of the keyboard.
Notes on the treble staff are usually played with the *right* hand.

Bass Clef – The *lower* part of the keyboard.
Notes on the bass staff are usually played with the *left* hand.

Piano music uses two staffs, as shown below.
The staffs are connected with a bracket called a **brace**.
Notice that **bar lines** also connect the two staffs.
A thick **double bar** is placed at the end of a piece of music.

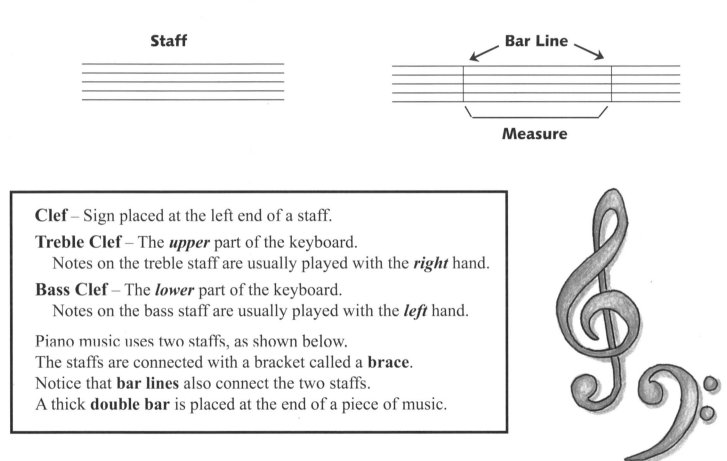

Treble Clef   **Double Bar**

Brace

Bar Lines

Bass Clef

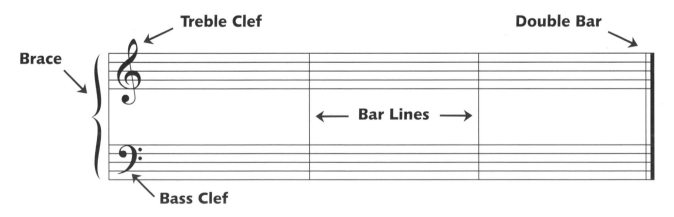

 This is Seymour (SEE-more) the note-watcher.
Seymour will call your attention to important things on each page from now on.

Musical Rhythm

Beat – A repeated equally-spaced movement in music. For example, the second hand of a clock moves with an even beat. The pulse of your heart is another example of a beat.

Rhythm – Movement of music going with a steady *beat*. Different kinds of music notes show the rhythm.

Note – Round symbol placed on or near a staff.

o ← **Whole Note** – Thick hollow note.
Named because it fills a *whole* measure in 4/4 time.

Quarter Note – Solid black note.
The short vertical line is called the *stem*.
The *note head* is the round part of the note.
The stem may go above or below the note head.

Time Signature – The two numbers at the beginning of a piece of music. For now, the UPPER number is the most important. It tells us that there are *4 beats* in each measure of 4/4 time.

$\frac{4}{4}$ ←

Counting – In 4/4 time, the beats of each measure are numbered 1-2-3-4.
♩ = 1 ← A *quarter* note gets **1** counting number.
A *whole* note gets **4** counting numbers.
o = 1-2-3-4 ← Counting numbers are printed directly below each arrow.

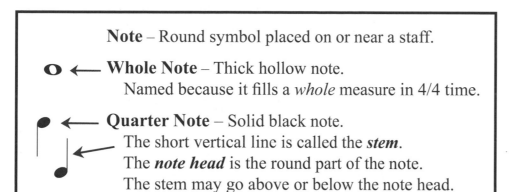

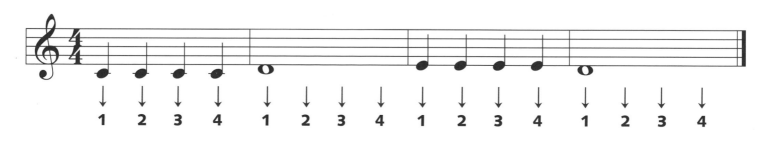

DIRECTIONS: Write the counting numbers 1, 2, 3 or 4, below each measure in the staff below. Write one number *directly below* each arrow. Look at the counting numbers above.

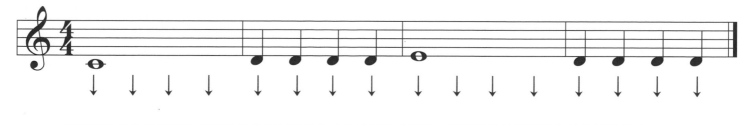

12

Equally Spaced Counting

 Equally spaced counting is very important in music because it makes a steady beat needed for all musical rhythms.

DIRECTIONS:

1. Write the counting numbers 1, 2, 3, or 4, below each measure in the staffs below. Write one number *directly below* each arrow. Notice that the arrows and numbers are *equally spaced*.

2. Say the counting numbers out loud. Try to keep the counts *equally spaced*, with the same amount of time for each number. After a few times, your teacher will clap the rhythm as you count, one clap for each note. Then you can try to clap for each note as your teacher counts.

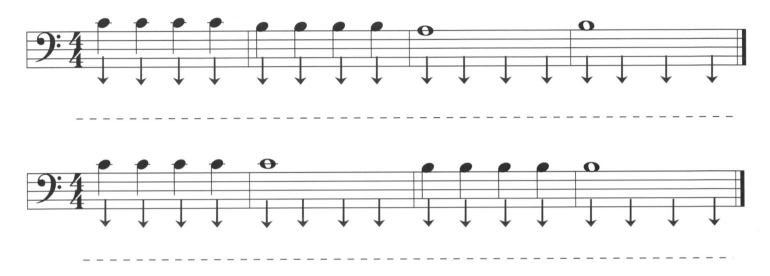

Music Puzzle

DIRECTIONS: Write the correct number in the box connected to each arrow below. Choose from the numbers printed here. Some numbers may be used twice.

Look at pages 10 and 11 for help in finding the answers.

1. Bar Line   **4.** Double Bar   **7.** Treble Clef
2. Bass Clef   **5.** Quarter Note   **8.** Whole Note
3. Brace   **6.** Time Signature

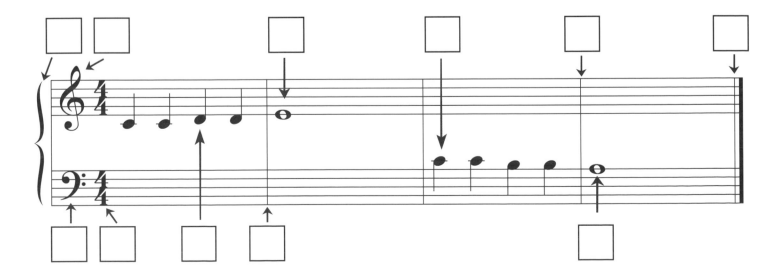

Finger Numbers

Left Hand Position

A B C
3 2 1

A B C

3 2 1 ← **Finger Numbers**

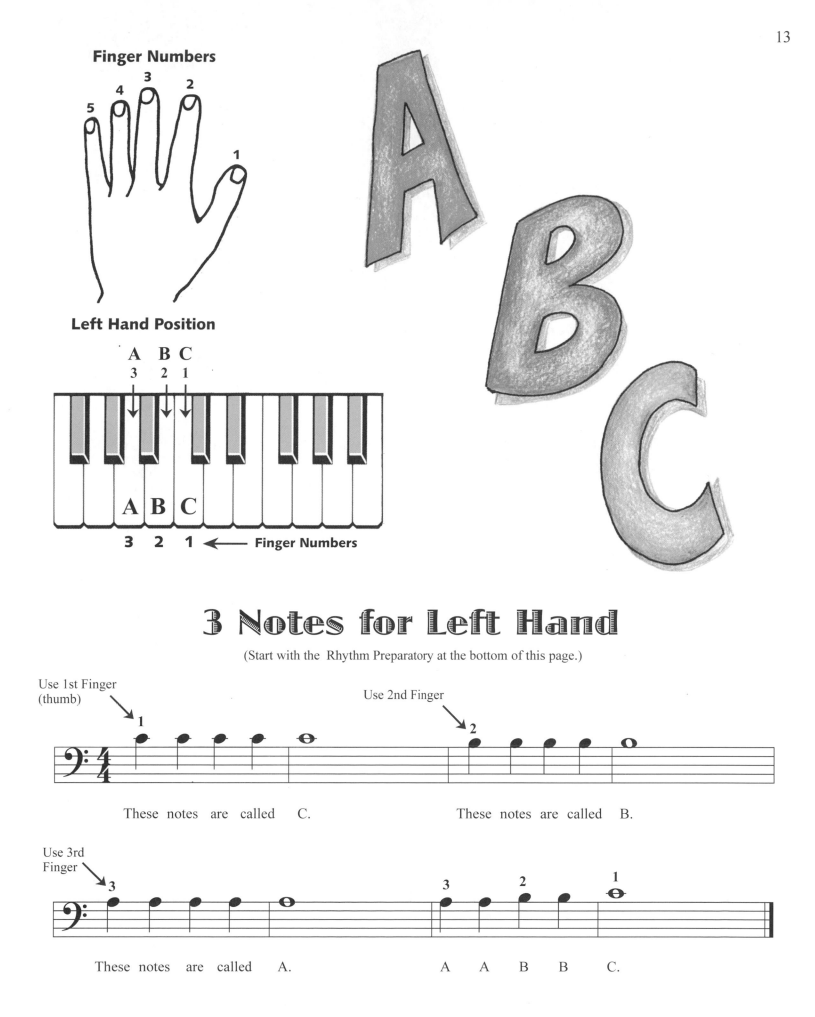

3 Notes for Left Hand

(Start with the Rhythm Preparatory at the bottom of this page.)

Use 1st Finger
(thumb)

Use 2nd Finger

These notes are called C.

These notes are called B.

Use 3rd
Finger

These notes are called A.

A A B B C.

Teacher's Rhythm Preparatory: (for pages 13 and 14)

The rhythm used here is the same as in the 2nd staff in the middle of page 12. Before starting this piece, ***demonstrate the rhythm*** by counting aloud and clapping, one clap for each note. Next, have the student count aloud as you clap for each note. Then, have the student clap for each note as you count. Finally, have the student count aloud and clap. Be sure the counting is evenly spaced.

Finger Numbers

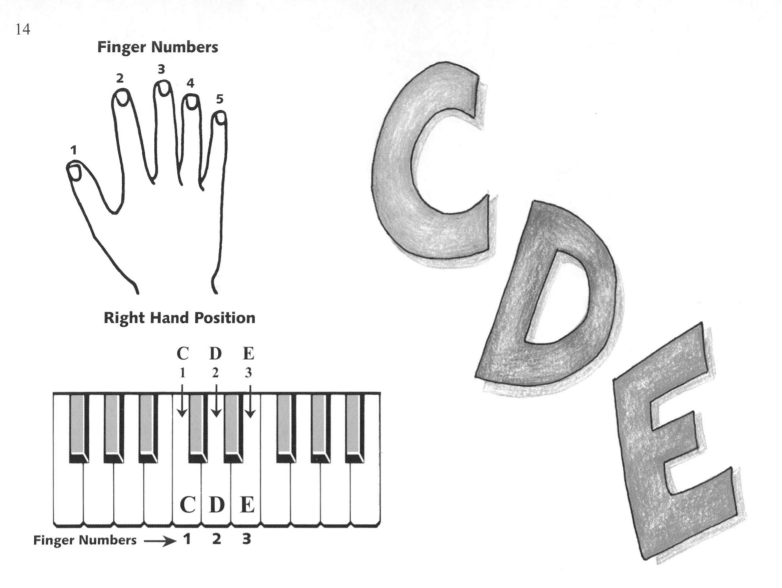

Right Hand Position

3 Notes for Right Hand

This piece uses the same rhythm as on page 13.

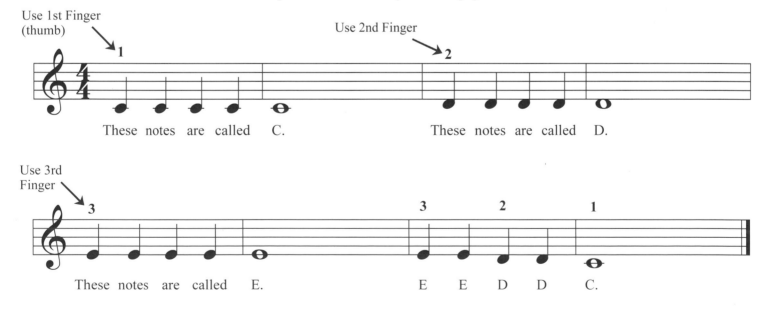

Use 1st Finger (thumb)

Use 2nd Finger

These notes are called C.

These notes are called D.

Use 3rd Finger

These notes are called E.

E E D D C.

Seymour (SEE-more)
the "Note Watcher" says:
"Try to keep your eyes *on the notes*."

Up, Down and Repeat

 Music notes may move UP or DOWN on the staff, like stair steps.
Music notes REPEAT when they stay straight across, on the *same line or space*.

DIRECTIONS: Write the word UP, DOWN or REPEAT in the box under each group of notes.
The first three boxes are samples.

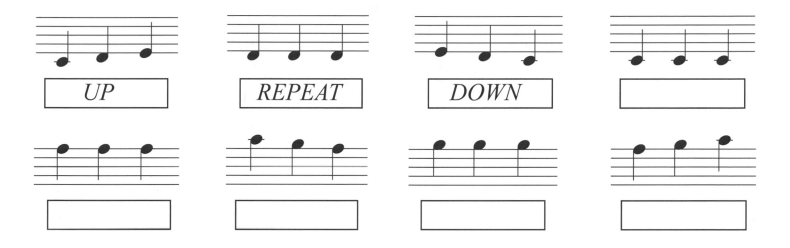

Line Notes and Space Notes

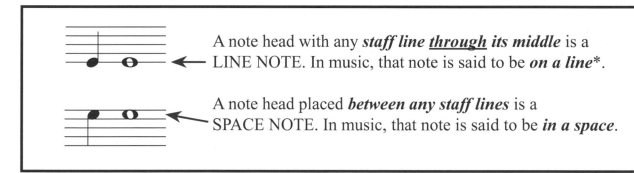

A note head with any *staff line __through__ its middle* is a
LINE NOTE. In music, that note is said to be *on a line**.

A note head placed *between any staff lines* is a
SPACE NOTE. In music, that note is said to be *in a space*.

DIRECTIONS: Write the word "line" or "space" in the box under each note below.
The first two boxes are samples.

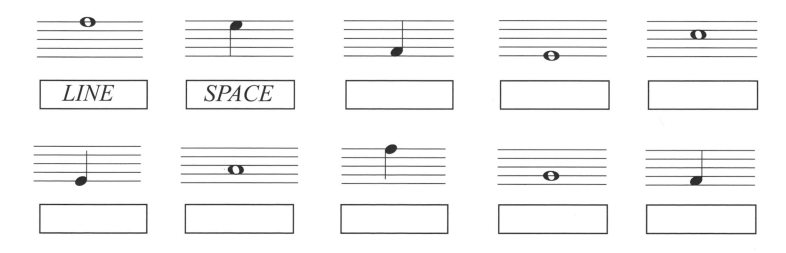

*A music note "on a line" is *different* than words written "on a line" (meaning just above the line).

Middle C is near the middle of the piano keyboard, close to the piano factory name.
Middle C can be a part of the treble staff or the bass staff.
It is always written on its own line, apart from the staffs.

 When close to the *top staff*, middle C is played with the RIGHT hand.

When close to the *bottom staff*, middle C is played with the LEFT hand.

See the Sea Lions

(See the C Lines)

Teacher's Note: You may begin using some of the *Note Finding Games* on page 49.

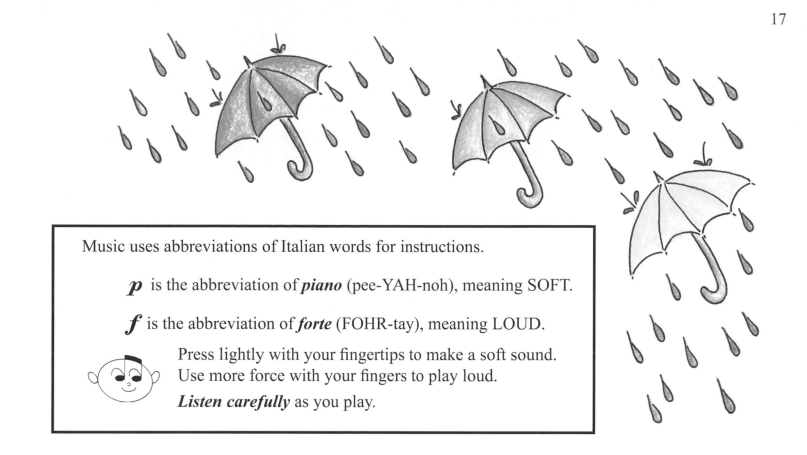

Music uses abbreviations of Italian words for instructions.

p is the abbreviation of **piano** (pee-YAH-noh), meaning SOFT.

f is the abbreviation of **forte** (FOHR-tay), meaning LOUD.

Press lightly with your fingertips to make a soft sound.
Use more force with your fingers to play loud.
Listen carefully as you play.

Rain

Words adapted from
Robert Louis Stevenson

Rain is rain - ing   all a - round, It   falls   on   flow - ers,   grass and tree. It

p

(play *softly*)

rains   on   the   um - brel - las here, And   on   the   ships   at   sea.

f

(play *loudly*)

Accompaniment:

Teacher's Note: Dynamic marks are presented as an opportunity for ear training and development of the sense of touch. Encourage the student to **listen carefully**, to coordinate ear and fingers while playing loud and soft.

This is a **HALF NOTE**. It has a hollow head.
The stem may go above or below the note head.

= 1-2   The half note gets **TWO** counting numbers.

Here are the counting numbers for the first four measures:

1 2 3 4   1 2 3 4   1 2 3 4   1 2 3 4

Football Tactics

(Start with the Rhythm Preparatory at the bottom of this page.)

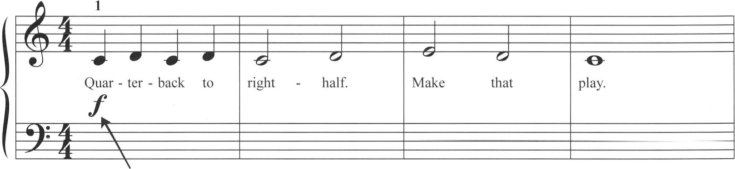

Quar - ter - back to   right - half.   Make   that   play.

f

(play *loudly*)

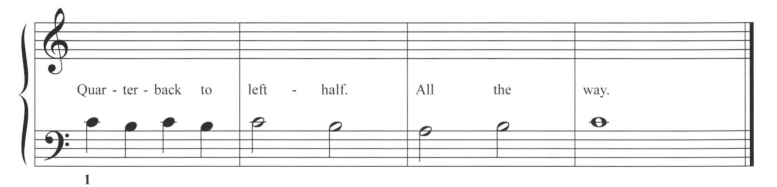

Quar - ter - back to   left - half.   All   the   way.

Accompaniment: *(Double bar indicates start of 2nd line of music.)*

Teacher's Rhythm Preparatory:
Before starting this piece, ***demonstrate the rhythm*** by counting aloud and clapping, one clap for each note.
Next, have the student count aloud as you clap for each note. Then, have the student clap for each note as you count.
Finally, have the student count aloud and clap. Be sure the ***counting is evenly spaced***.

Slur – The slur is a curved line that joins a group of notes to form a musical thought. Slurs may be placed above or below the notes.

Melody Patterns – Slurs help us find patterns in the melody. Here are two melody patterns, one in the treble staff and one in the bass staff.

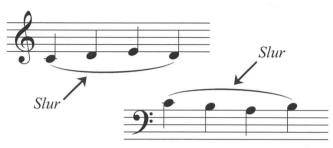

Slur

Slur

In the piece, "Revolving Door," the melody pattern in the treble staff is shown with the *number 1* in a circle. This pattern is *used three times*. The melody pattern in the bass staff is also used three times. The bass pattern is shown with a *number 2* in a circle.

Revolving Door

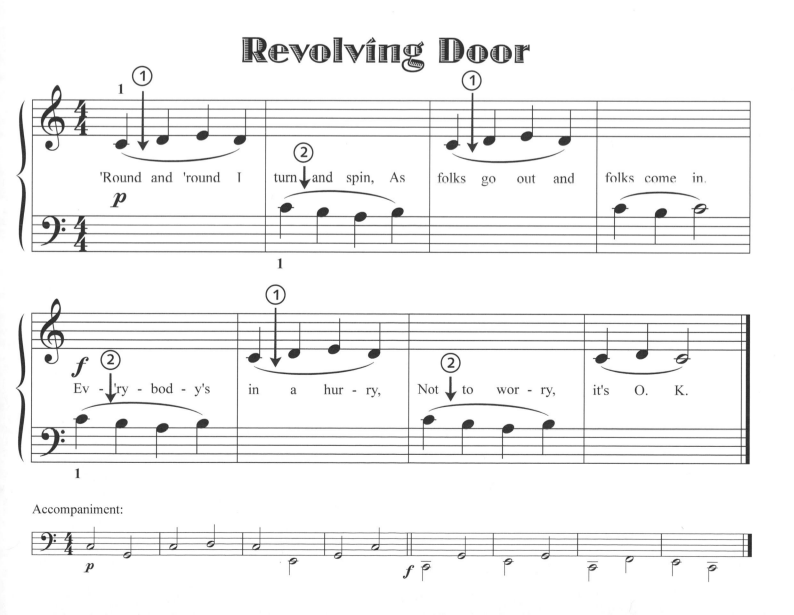

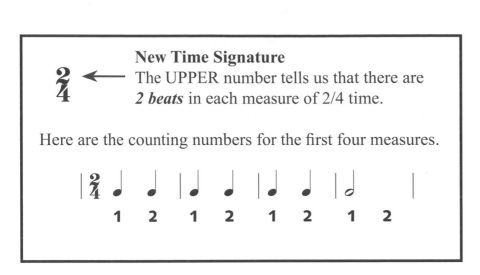

New Time Signature

2/4 ← The UPPER number tells us that there are *2 beats* in each measure of 2/4 time.

Here are the counting numbers for the first four measures.

Three Strikes and Out

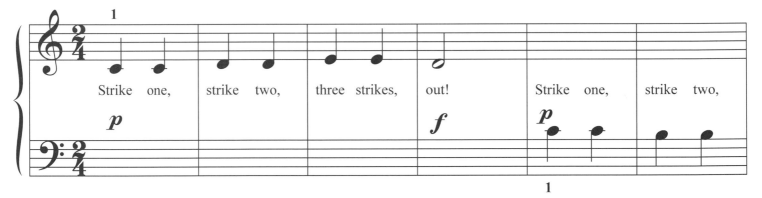

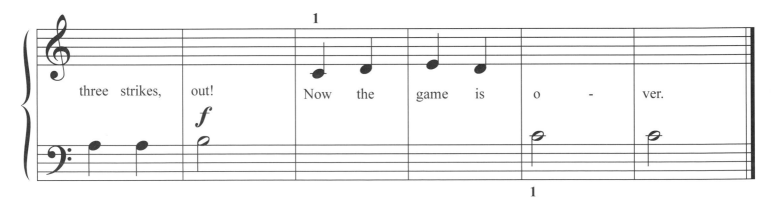

Accompaniment:

Rhythm Patterns – Slurs help us to find patterns in the rhythm. This piece has **three slurs**. The **rhythm is the same** in each slur group, but the notes are different.

Notice that the 2nd slur starts in the right hand and continues in the left hand in the bottom line of music.

Two New Notes – **G** in Left hand – **F** in Right hand

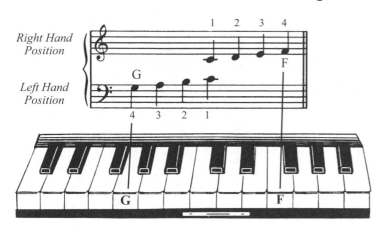

Tom and Tess Thumb

New Note, F

Tom   Thumb,   play   the   drum.   Tess   Thumb,

f   *p*

Slur continued from end of line above.

play   the   drum.   Tom,   Tess,   play   the   drum!

f

New Note, G

Accompaniment:

22

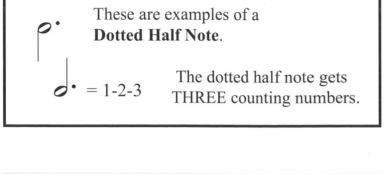

These are examples of a **Dotted Half Note**.

𝅗𝅥· = 1-2-3   The dotted half note gets THREE counting numbers.

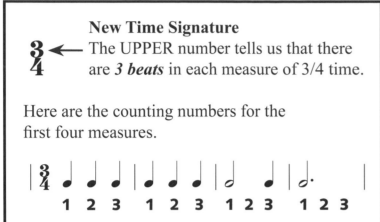

New Time Signature

3/4 ← The UPPER number tells us that there are *3 beats* in each measure of 3/4 time.

Here are the counting numbers for the first four measures.

1 2 3   1 2 3   1 2 3   1 2 3

Paladîn

Dotted Half Note

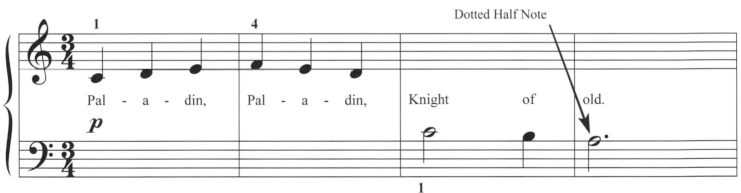

Pal - a - din,   Pal - a - din,   Knight   of   old.

p

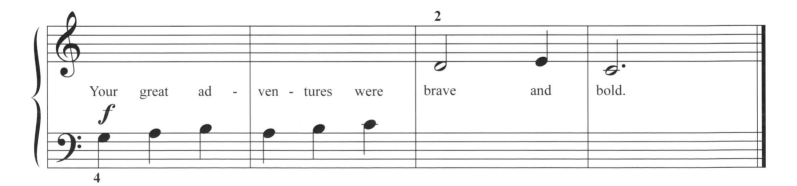

Your great ad - ven - tures were   brave   and   bold.

f

Accompaniment:

p   *f*

Teacher's Note: You may continue using some of the *Note Finding Games* on page 49.

Review means to play pieces you have learned before.
Review practice will improve your playing.
Here are some things to try during review practice.

1. Be sure the counting is *evenly spaced*.
2. Play measures *loud and soft* as marked.
3. Play *without looking at the music* (optional).

Flight Attendant

Fas - ten your seat belts, we're tak - ing off soon.

p

Flight time is short, we'll ar - rive be - fore noon.

f

Accompaniment:

p   *f*

*Interval – An interval is the distance from one note to another. The ***interval number*** is the same as the number of ***alphabet letters*** from one note to another note.

For example, A to B is a ***2nd***, because the distance is ***2 alphabet letters*** (A-B).

C to D is also a ***2nd***, because the distance is 2 alphabet letters (C-D).

A to C is a ***3rd***, because the distance is ***3 alphabet letters*** (A-B-C).

Learning to recognize different intervals will help you to read music more easily.
Here are examples of intervals used in "Flight 88." Notice that intervals can move up or down.

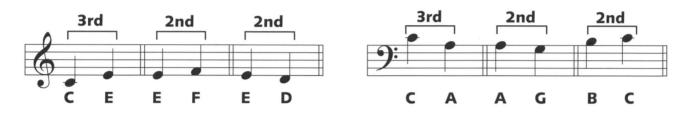

Flight 88

3rds are shown by arrows. All other intervals are 2nds.

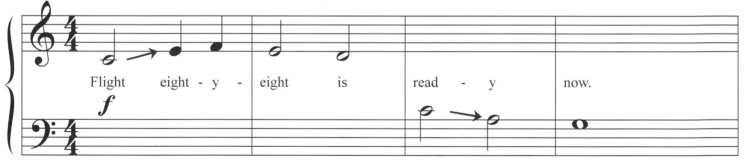

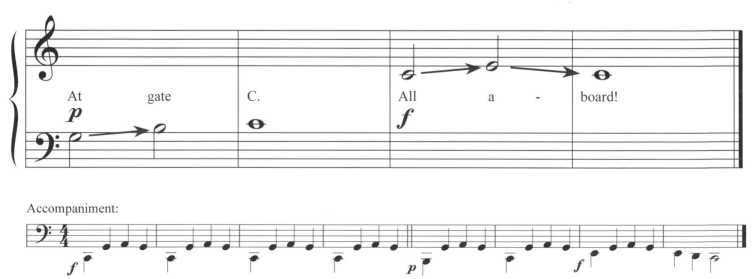

Accompaniment:

* Teacher's Note: These are simple white key intervals. Explanation of major and minor intervals should come later.

3rds Between Staffs – Here are examples of intervals of a 3rd between the treble staff and bass staff. Each 3rd is shown with an arrow connecting the two notes. The distance between the two notes looks greater because of the skip from one staff to another, but the distance is still *3 alphabet letters*.

Notice that in these measures, the notes of each 3rd change from one hand to the other.

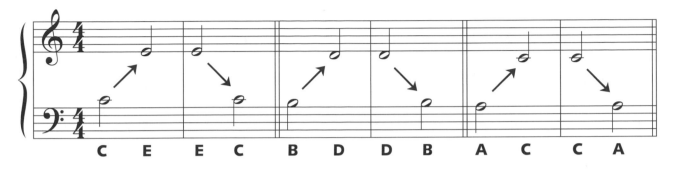

Computers

3rds between staffs are shown with arrows. Can you find four *other* 3rds?

Words by Joan Cupp

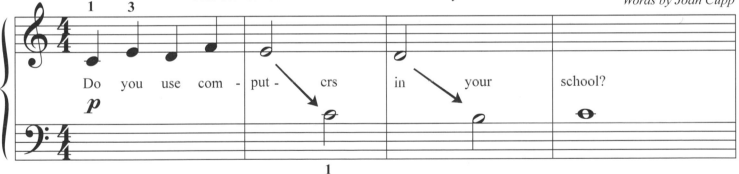

Do you use com - put - ers in your school?

Click a - way to find things, that's so cool.

Accompaniment:

Two New Notes:

F in Left hand – G in Right hand

Glittering Goldfish

Draw a circle around all the new notes: G in the right hand, F in left hand.

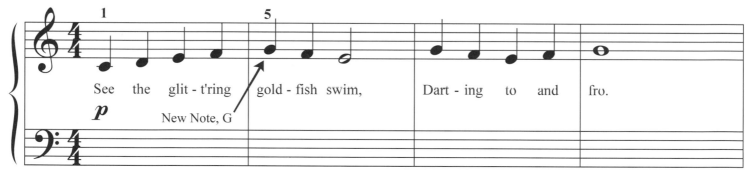

See the glit - t'ring gold - fish swim, Dart - ing to and fro.

p

New Note, G

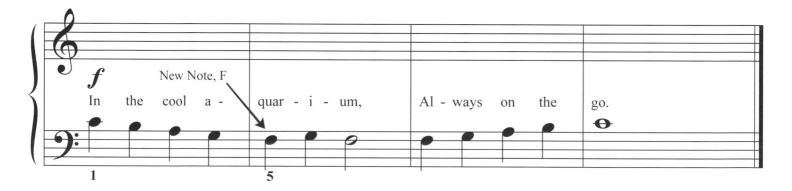

f

New Note, F

In the cool a - quar - i - um, Al - ways on the go.

Accompaniment:

p   *f*

4th and 5th Intervals – The "Weather Man" uses these new intervals:

G to D is a *5th*, because the distance is *5 alphabet letters* (G-A-B-C-D).

C to F is a *4th*, because the distance is *4 alphabet letters* (C-D-E-F).

A to D is also a *4th*, because the distance is 4 alphabet letters (A-B-C-D).

Rest – Rests are signs used for *silence*. They show places where *nothing* is played. During a rest, keep your hand in position over the keyboard.

Rests are named and counted the same as notes.

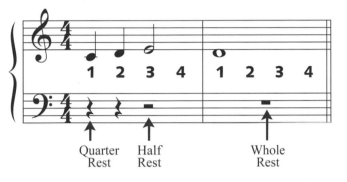

Quarter Rest   Half Rest   Whole Rest

The half rest and whole rest look almost alike.

The **half** rest is *above* the 3rd staff line.

The **whole** rest is *below* the 4th staff line.

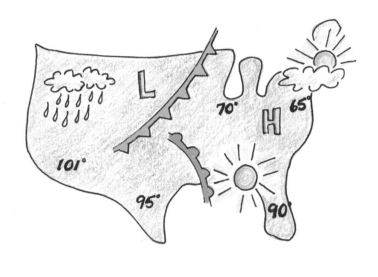

Weather Man

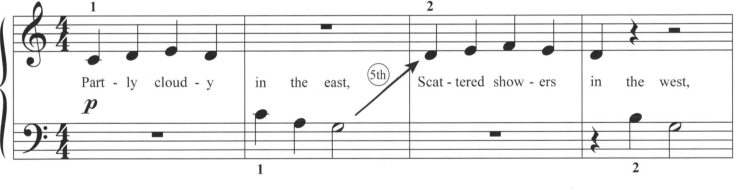

Part - ly cloud - y   in the east, (5th)   Scat - tered show - ers   in the west,

Warm down south and   cool up north, But   fair's the weath - er   I like best.

Accompaniment:

Pickup Note – The note at the beginning of this piece is alone in a measure with only one beat. It is called a *pickup note*. It may also be called an "upbeat note."

Notice the counting numbers below. The pickup note is on count 3. The note in the last measure gets counts 1 and 2. If you add the counts in the first and last measures together, the total will be 3 – a full measure.

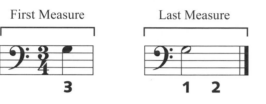

Ice Skating

Circled numbers show slurs connecting two different melody patterns. Notice how these two patterns are repeated.

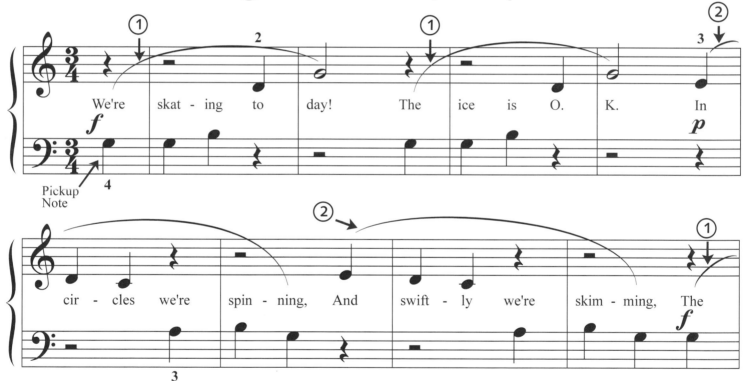

We're skat - ing to day! The ice is O. K. In

cir - cles we're spin - ning, And swift - ly we're skim - ming, The

ice is O. K. We're skat - ing to - day.

Accompaniment:

4/4 Pickup Note – This piece begins with a pickup note in the first measure.

Notice the counting numbers below. The pickup note is on count 4. The notes in the last measure get counts 1, 2, and 3. If you add the counts in the first and last measures together, the total will be 4 counts.

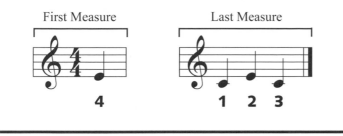

E-Mail

Pickup Note

Two melody patterns are the same. Can you find them?

Words suggested by Joan Cupp

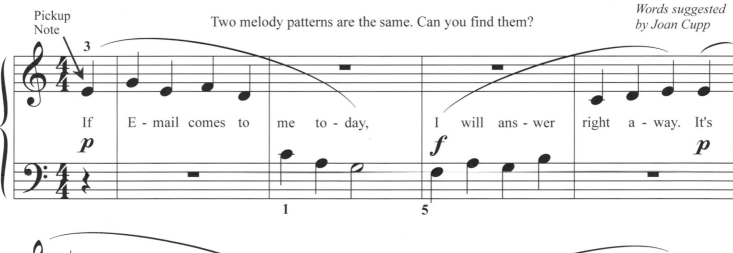

If E - mail comes to me to - day, I will ans - wer right a - way. It's

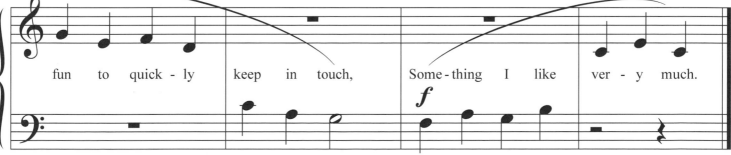

fun to quick - ly keep in touch, Some - thing I like ver - y much.

Accompaniment:

Teacher's Note: You may continue using some of the *Note Finding Games* on page 49.

Before starting to play a piece,
take a few seconds to look for:

Time signature

Finger numbers

Dynamics (loud and soft)

Rhythm (counting of notes and rests)

Also check to see which hand starts
playing first.

Twinkle, Twinkle Fifty Stars

Circled numbers show slurs connecting different melody patterns. Notice that these two patterns are repeated.

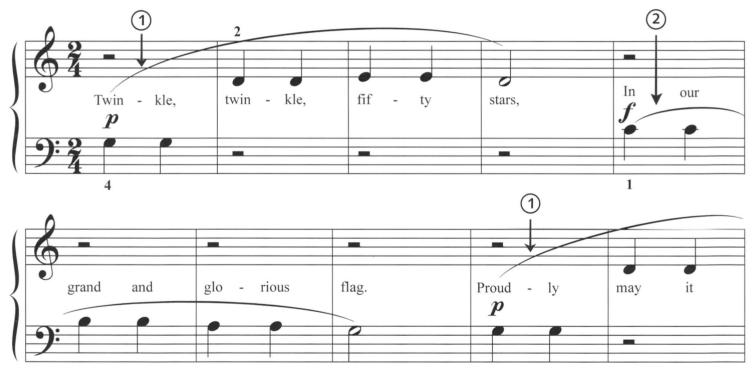

Twin - kle, twinkle, fif - ty stars, In our

grand and glo - rious flag. Proud - ly may it

al - ways wave, Sym - bol of the free and brave.

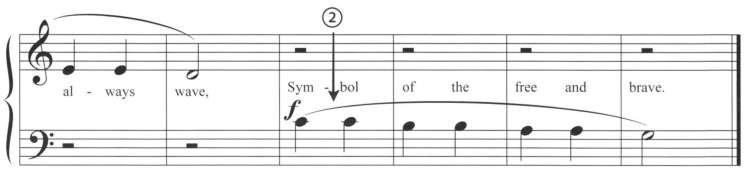

Accompaniment:

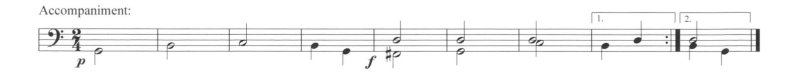

Making Music Quiz

DIRECTIONS: Draw a circle around each correct answer below. The first line is a sample.

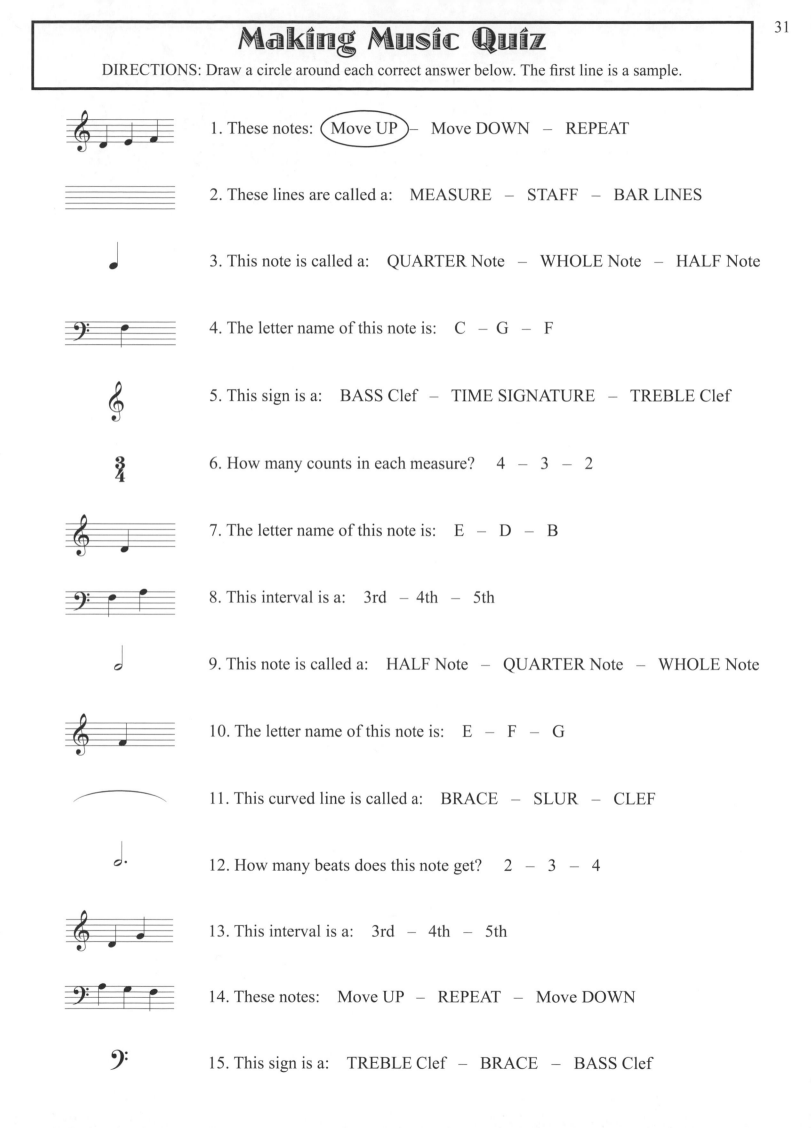

1. These notes: (Move UP) – Move DOWN – REPEAT

2. These lines are called a: MEASURE – STAFF – BAR LINES

3. This note is called a: QUARTER Note – WHOLE Note – HALF Note

4. The letter name of this note is: C – G – F

5. This sign is a: BASS Clef – TIME SIGNATURE – TREBLE Clef

6. How many counts in each measure? 4 – 3 – 2

7. The letter name of this note is: E – D – B

8. This interval is a: 3rd – 4th – 5th

9. This note is called a: HALF Note – QUARTER Note – WHOLE Note

10. The letter name of this note is: E – F – G

11. This curved line is called a: BRACE – SLUR – CLEF

12. How many beats does this note get? 2 – 3 – 4

13. This interval is a: 3rd – 4th – 5th

14. These notes: Move UP – REPEAT – Move DOWN

15. This sign is a: TREBLE Clef – BRACE – BASS Clef

32

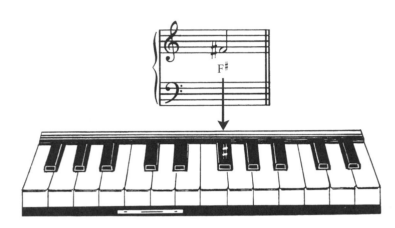

Thanksgiving Day Parade

Look at the slurs that show melody patterns. Can you find two patterns that are the same?

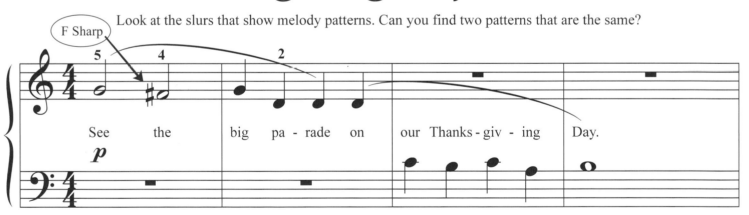

See the big pa - rade on our Thanks - giv - ing Day.

p

Soon will come the great De - cem - ber Hol - i - days.

f

Accompaniment:

p   *f*

Key Signature – The sharp sign, next to the clef at the beginning of each staff, is called a *key signature*.

In this piece, it means that *every F* should be played *sharp*.

Snow Man

Key Signature:
F Sharp

This piece has three F's that should be played *sharp*. Can you find them?

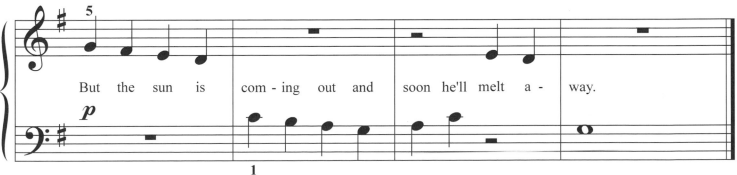

Accompaniment:

Sound of Music

Look at the slurs that show melody patterns. Which patterns are the same?

French Folk Tune

Both hands play together

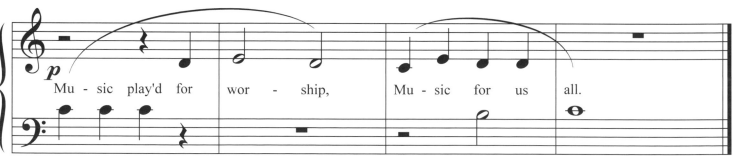

Accompaniment:

Teacher's Note: Finger numbers have been omitted in this piece to make sure that the student will read *notes, not finger numbers*.

Three C's – This piece has three different C's:
  1. Middle C
  2. C *below* Middle C (in the bass staff)
  3. C *above* Middle C (in the treble staff)
Notice where each C is located in the staffs below.

In "Roger and Over" each hand *crosses over* to play the lower and upper C's.

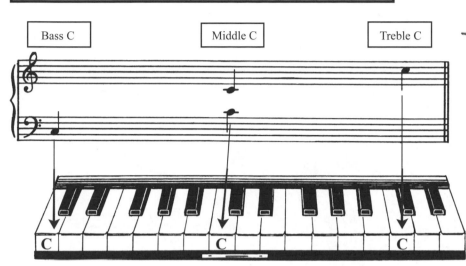

Roger and Over

"Roger and Over" is a military phrase meaning "message received, I understand."

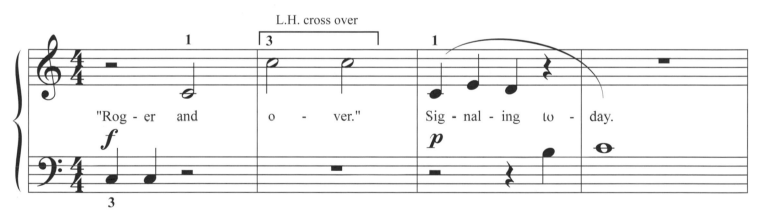

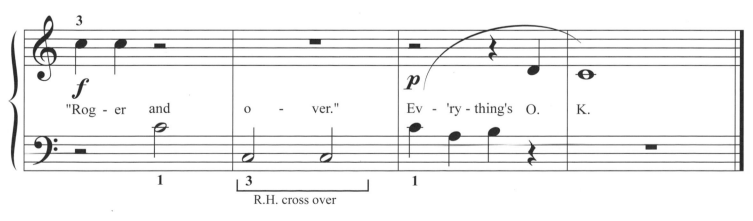

Accompaniment:

Looking Ahead – It's a good idea to try to look at *two or three notes at a time*, rather than one note at a time.
Here are some things to look for as you go ahead:

    Note movement: Up, Down or Repeat
    Different Intervals
    Fingering
    Changes from one staff to another
    Note values and counting

Looking ahead will help make it easier to read the music correctly as you play.

September Song

This piece has 13 intervals of a 3rd in it. Can you find them?

Accompaniment:

Eighth Note Pairs – The heavy line connecting the stems of two 8th notes is called a *beam*. Without the beam, they would be quarter notes.

Two 8th notes together get ONE counting number, the same as a quarter note.

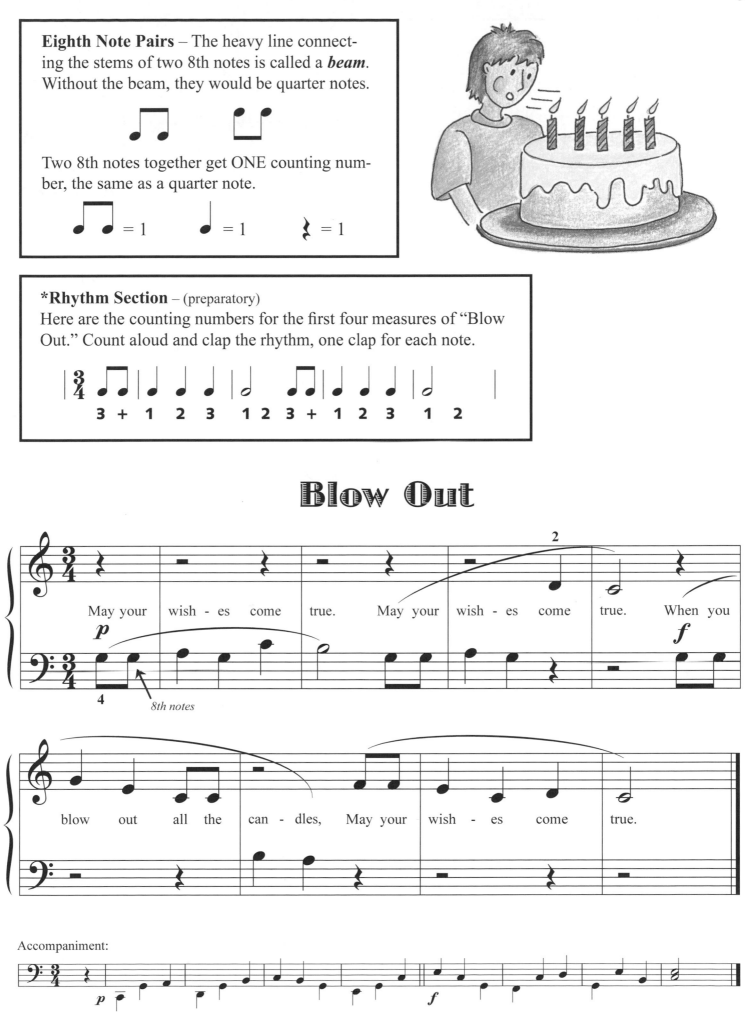

*Rhythm Section – (preparatory)
Here are the counting numbers for the first four measures of "Blow Out." Count aloud and clap the rhythm, one clap for each note.

3 + 1 2 3 1 2 3 + 1 2 3 1 2

Blow Out

May your wish - es come true. May your wish - es come true. When you

p

f

4

8th notes

blow out all the can - dles, May your wish - es come true.

Accompaniment:

p

f

* Teacher's Note: The student will probably recognize the melody used here. Be sure that the rhythm for the two 8th notes is correct – **not like a dotted 8th and 16th**. The plus sign is used as an abbreviation for "and."

38

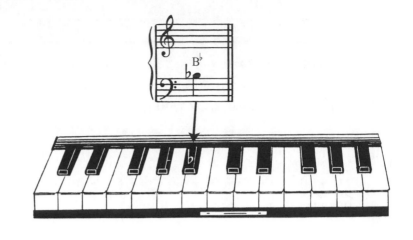

Window Shopping

Look at the slurs that show the melody patterns. Can you find patterns that are the same?

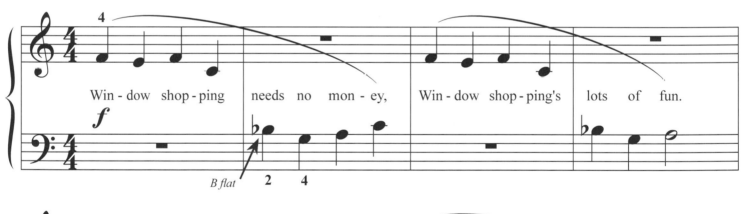

Win - dow shop - ping needs no mon - ey, Win - dow shop - ping's lots of fun.

B flat

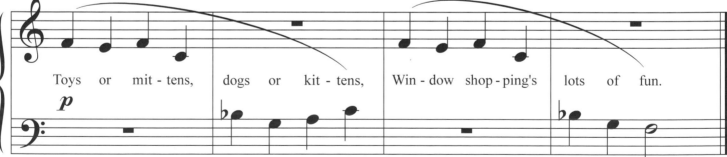

Toys or mit - tens, dogs or kit - tens, Win - dow shop - ping's lots of fun.

Accompaniment:

* **Teacher's Note:** Be sure the student understands that an accidental flat or sharp is
always placed to the *LEFT of a note*, and to the *RIGHT of a letter*.

New Key Signature – The flat sign, next to the clef at the beginning of each staff, is another *key signature*.

It means that *every B* in the piece should be played *flat*.

Covered Wagons

This piece has four B's that should be played *flat*. Can you find them?

Adapted from
Carl Maria von Weber

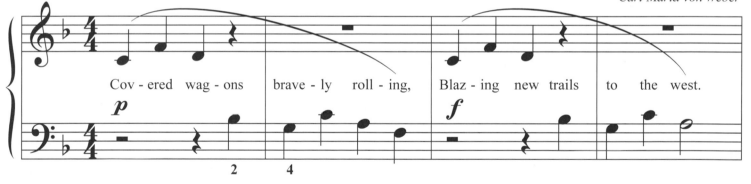

Cov - ered wag - ons brave - ly roll - ing, Blaz - ing new trails to the west.

'Round the camp - fire in the eve - ning, Pi - o - neers would stop and rest.

Accompaniment:

Broken Chord – A chord is made of three or more notes that are played at the same time.
When the notes of a chord are played one at a time, it is called a *broken chord*.
Below are the notes for three chords, **C**, **F** and **G**. Each chord is named after the bottom note.

C chord:

C E G   C E G

F chord:

F A C   F A C

G chord:

G B D   G B D

Ranger Station C

C Major broken chords, going up and down, are shown with brackets.
A new bass note is shown with an arrow. Find this note on the keyboard diagram on the front inside cover of this book.

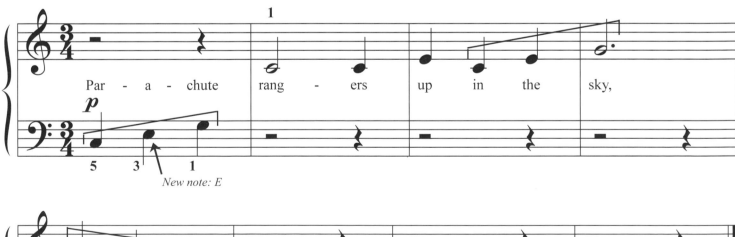

Par - a - chute   rang - ers   up   in   the   sky,

p

5   3   1

New note: E

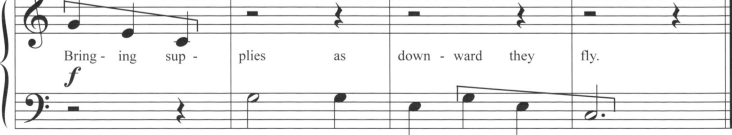

Bring - ing   sup -   plies   as   down - ward   they   fly.

f

Ranger Station F

F Major broken chords, going up and down, are shown with brackets.

A new treble note is shown with an arrow. Find this note on the keyboard diagram on the front inside cover of this book.

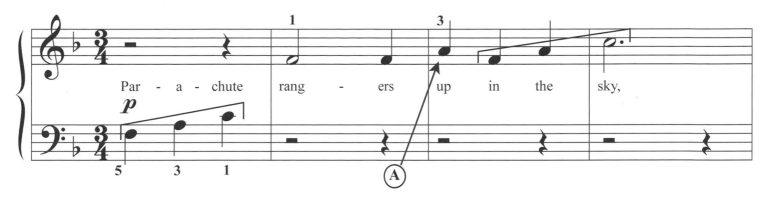

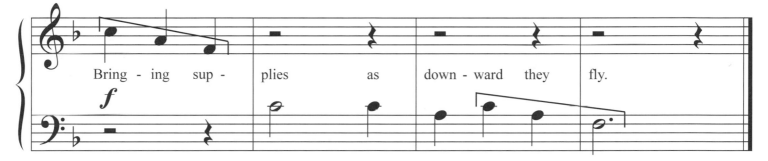

Ranger Station G

G Major broken chords, going up and down, are shown with brackets.

Three new notes are shown with arrows. Find the notes on the keyboard diagram on the front inside cover.

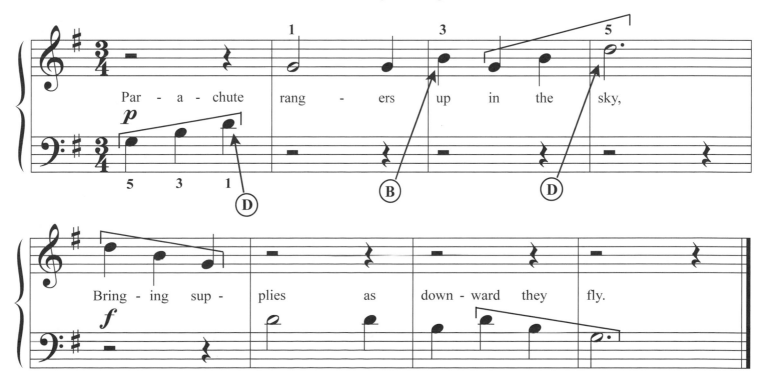

42

The Whale

Can you find the three *natural* signs in this piece?

Accompaniment:

* The natural also cancels out a sharp or flat in the key signature.

Dissonance – Music may have strange, harsh sounds called *dissonance*. In "Skeeters Waltz," dissonance is used to show the buzzing and biting of mosquitoes.

Whole Rest = Whole Measure – A whole rest may be used in *any whole* measure. In this piece, the whole rest gets *3 counting numbers* because the time signature is 3/4.

Reminder Accidental – A parenthesis shows that an accidental is being used as a reminder.

(♯)　　(♭)　　(♮)

Skeeter's Waltz

Notes with a circle are also changed by the accidental sharp or flat on the note before.
Be sure to hold each dotted half note for a *full three beats*.

Amos Quito

Whole Rest is used for a whole measure.

Reminder accidental

Accompaniment:

Cat and Mouse

French Folk Tune

New hand position

Tom - my is af - ter me what shall I do? Here's an es -

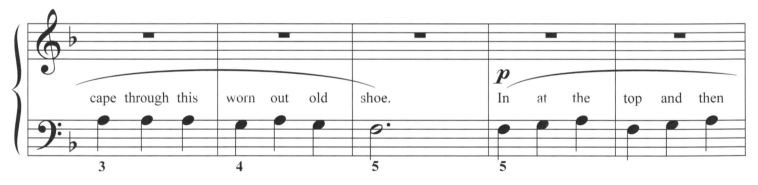

cape through this worn out old shoe. In at the top and then

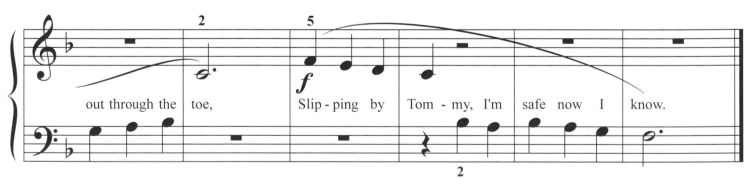

out through the toe, Slip - ping by Tom - my, I'm safe now I know.

Accompaniment:

Slurs help us to find *melody patterns* and *rhythm patterns*. This piece has four slurs.
Some of the slurs are continued from one line to the next. Find the first note of each slur.

The *melody pattern is the same* in two of the slurs. Can you find them?

The *rhythm pattern is the same* in each slur group, but the notes are different.

Burgers

Irish Folk Tune

Fresh oat - burg - ers are the food hors - es all eat, And worm - burg - ers

give the red rob - ins a treat. Green grass - burg - ers are a great

fav - 'rite with cows, But give me a ham - burg - er sand - wich right now!

Accompaniment:

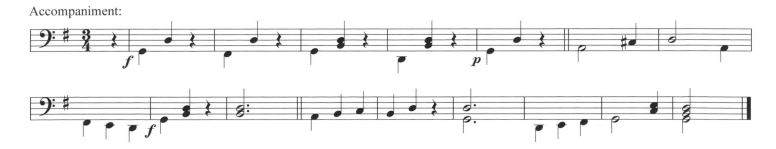

Staccato – A dot *above or below* a note head is called *staccato*. It means to play with a short touch, as though you were touching something hot.

In this piece, *all right hand notes* are played staccato.

Notice that the dot for a dotted half note is *beside* the note. The dot for a staccato note is *above or below* the note.

Two Notes Played Together
When two notes share the same stem, both notes should be played at the *same time*.

The notes in the treble staff are an interval of a 2nd.

These notes have a *dissonant* sound, which imitates the chirp of a cricket.

The Cricket and the Bumble Bee

The right hand plays *softly* for the cricket. The left hand plays *loudly* for the bumble bee.

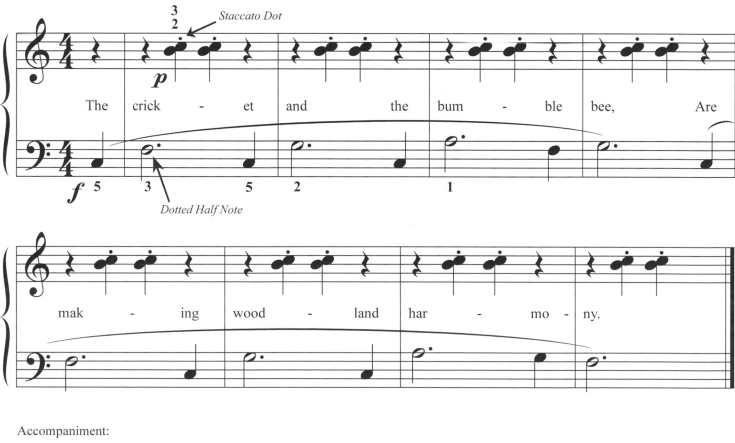

The crick - et and the bum - ble bee, Are

mak - ing wood - land har - mo - ny.

Accompaniment:

Certificate of Progress

This certifies that

_____

has successfully completed

PRIMER LEVEL

of the Schaum

Making Music Method

and is eligible for advancement to
LEVEL ONE

_____
Teacher

_____
Date

Schaum Music Dictionary

Also see Reference Page on the front inside cover.

Terms listed here are limited to those commonly found in Primer Level books. These definitions are purposely brief. For more details see the page numbers listed.

The accented syllable is shown in capital letters.

accidental (ack-sih-DEN-tal) A sharp, flat or natural that is not in a key signature. See pages 42 and 43.

bar line Vertical line placed in the staff. See page 10.

bass clef Indicates the *lower* part of the keyboard, middle C and *below*. See page 10.

beam Heavy line connecting the stems of 8th notes. See page 37.

beat Repeated equally-spaced movement in music. See page 11.

brace Bracket used to join two staffs. See page 10.

broken chord Notes of a chord that are played one at a time. See page 40.

chord (KORD) Three or more notes that are played at the same time. See page 40.

clef Musical sign placed at the left end of a staff. See page 10.

dissonance (DISS-uh-nunce) Intervals or chords that sound strange, unpleasant or harsh. See pages 43 and 46.

dotted half note Half note with a dot added. See page 22.

double bar Is placed at the end of a piece of music. See page 10.

8th notes The stems of two quarter notes that are connected with a beam. See page 37.

flat [♭] Means to go *down* to the nearest key. See page 38.

f Abbreviation of *forte* (FOHR-tay), meaning loud. See page 17.

half note Note with a stem and hollow note head. See page 18.

half rest Rest placed *above* the 3rd staff line. See page 27.

interval The distance from one note to another. See pages 24, 25 and 27.

key signature Sharps or flats next to the clef at the beginning of a staff. See pages 33 and 39.

line note Note head with any staff line through its middle. See page 15.

measure Part of the staff between two bar lines. See page 10.

melody pattern Group of notes shown by a slur. See pages 19, 28, 30 and 45.

middle C The C near the middle of the keyboard, close to the piano factory name. See page 16.

natural [♮] Cancels a sharp or flat. See page 42.

note Round symbol placed on or near a staff. See page 11.

note head Round part of a note. See page 11

p Abbreviation of *piano* (pee-YAH-noh), meaning soft. See page 17.

pickup note Note at the beginning of a piece, alone in a measure. See pages 28, 29, 37, 42, 45 and 46.

quarter note Note with a stem and black note head. See page 11.

reminder accidental Parenthesis shows the accidental is used as a reminder. See page 43.

rest Sign used for silence. See pages 27 and 43.

rhythm Movement of music going with a steady beat. See page 11.

rhythm pattern Group of notes shown with a slur. See pages 21 and 45.

sharp [♯] Means to go *up* to the nearest key. See page 32.

slur Curved line that joins a group of notes to form a musical thought. See pages 19, 21 and 45.

space note A note head placed between any staff lines. See page 15.

staccato (stah-KAH-toh) Dot above or below a note. The note is played with a short touch. See page 46.

staff Group of five equally spaced horizontal lines on which music notes are placed. See page 10.

stem Short vertical line attached to a note head. May go above or below the note head. See page 11.

time signature Two numbers at the beginning of a piece of music. See pages 11, 20 and 22.

treble clef Indicates the *upper* part of the keyboard, middle C and *above*. See page 10.

upbeat note (UP-beet) Same as a pickup note. See page 28.

whole note Note with thick note head and no stem. See page 11.

whole rest Rest placed *below* the 4th staff line. See pages 27 and 43.